# COPING WITH A DISABILITY

## BY HOLLY DUHIG

**BookLife**
**PUBLISHING**

©2018
**BookLife Publishing**
**King's Lynn**
**Norfolk PE30 4LS**

All rights reserved.
Printed in Malaysia.

A catalogue record for this book is available from the British Library.

**ISBN:** 978-1-78637-292-5

**Written by:**
Holly Duhig

**Edited by:**
Kirsty Holmes

**Designed by:**
Danielle Rippengill

**Image Credits**

*All images are courtesy of Shutterstock.com, unless otherwise specified. With thanks to Getty Images, Thinkstock Photo and iStockphoto. Front Cover – Jaren Jai Wicklund, prapann, Alexander Lysenko, Mc Satori, Ambient Ideas, Ortis, xpixel. Images used on every spread – Red_Spruce, MG Drachal, Alexander Lysenko, Kues, Flas100, Kanate. 1 – prapann. 1 & 2 – Jaren Jai Wicklund. 4 – Jaren Jai Wicklund, claire norman, Nikolaeva. 5 – 1000 Words, Jaren Jai Wicklund. 6 & 7 – Jaren Jai Wicklund, Nikolaeva. 8 & 9 – Jaren Jai Wicklund. 10 – redchocolate, alexandre zveiger, SORNDA, Nikolaeva. 11, 12 & 13 – Jaren Jai Wicklund. 14 – redchocolate, Olesia Bilkei, Jaren Jai Wicklund. 15 – Monkey Business Images, Nikolaeva. 16 – Jaren Jai Wicklund. 17 – Andrey_Popov. 18, 19, 20, 22 & 23 – Jaren Jai Wicklund. 21 – Lorena Fernandez.*

# CONTENTS

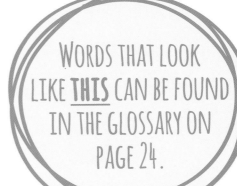

WORDS THAT LOOK LIKE **THIS** CAN BE FOUND IN THE GLOSSARY ON PAGE 24.

# My Family

KAT

DAD

MAYA

ME

My two dogs,
Tilly and Trish.

My name is Finn. I live with my dad and my two sisters,
Kat and Maya. My dad's name is George.

My dad, Maya and I live in a **bungalow** with a big garden.
My oldest sister Kat has moved out and lives on her own now.

My Big Sister

Our House

I USE A WHEELCHAIR, SO HAVING A BUNGALOW MAKES IT EASIER TO GET AROUND.

# HAVING A DISABILITY

I have a disability called cerebral palsy, or CP for short. A disability is when something in your body or brain doesn't work properly, which makes doing certain things more difficult.

I SOMETIMES USE ARM BRACES AND A MOUTH GUARD TO HELP ME.

Having CP means my brain finds it hard to send the right messages to the **muscles** in my body. Because of this, it's hard for me to control the way my body moves.

Some things that are easy for other people can be quite hard for me. My dad helps me use my knife and fork at dinner times because holding them can be difficult.

CP also makes walking difficult. This is why I use a wheelchair. I love my wheelchair. It is **motorised** so I can move it wherever I want.

RAMP

My house has everything I need – it's great! The doors and hallways are nice and wide so that I can move my wheelchair around easily. My front door has a ramp so that I can get in and out by myself.

In my bedroom, I have lots of toys on a big play-mat. My favourite toys are my cars. I was given lots of cars on my birthday!

I ALSO HAVE LOTS OF BOOKS. I WANT TO BE A FAMOUS AUTHOR ONE DAY.

# Out and About

On weekends, we go on family days out. Some days we go to the beach and other days we go to the park. I like playing on the swings.

This swing was made for children with disabilities like me.

On Sundays, we go to visit my grandad at his house and have a family dinner. Grandad has **arthritis** so he uses a wheelchair too!

# At School

JULIAN

On weekdays, I get taken to school in a bus which has a special wheelchair lift. My friend Julian also gets this bus. He uses a walking frame.

A lady called Mary-Anne helps me with my school work. She is my **scribe**. I tell her what I want to write and she copies it into my workbook.

MARY-ANNE

MY FAVOURITE SUBJECT AT SCHOOL IS HISTORY.

CP means that my muscles don't always listen to my brain. This can make talking hard work and it's sometimes difficult to make myself understood.

People often interrupt me. This is very frustrating.

GINA IS DEAF.
THIS MEANS SHE CAN'T
HEAR VERY WELL.

My best friend Gina uses **sign language**. She also finds it hard sometimes to get people to understand her. I am always **patient** with Gina.

# Answering Questions ⁇

Having a disability is unusual, so people often ask questions about it. Normally, I don't mind answering them – I find it interesting too!

I DON'T HAVE TO ANSWER QUESTIONS IF I DON'T WANT TO. SOME PEOPLE ARE TOO NOSY!

I don't like it when people only talk about my CP though. There's more to me than just my disability. I like talking to my friends about all sorts of things!

> I ALWAYS ASK IF I NEED HELP, BUT I CAN DO MOST THINGS ON MY OWN.

Because I'm in a wheelchair, people sometimes treat me like I can't do things by myself. Sometimes they talk down to me, or treat me like I'm younger than I am. This feels really hurtful.

To help me become able to do even more things by myself, I go to see a **physical therapist**. She teaches me **exercises** that keep my muscles strong and healthy. I practice these at home too.

I might have CP but that's just one part of me. I also have lots of fun with my friends and family, and I love reading history books.

Everybody has things about them that make them different. Having a disability is just one of those things. We should celebrate our differences!

# Glossary and Index

## Glossary

| | |
|---|---|
| arthritis | a disease which causes pain and stiffness in the body's joints |
| bungalow | a type of building which has all the rooms on one floor and no stairs |
| exercises | activities that require physical effort |
| motorised | fitted with a motor or engine |
| muscles | bundles of tissue in the body that help you move |
| patient | calm and respectful |
| physical therapist | a person who is trained to treat problems with muscles and joints |
| scribe | a person who writes on behalf of someone else |
| sign language | a system of communication used by deaf people, using hand movements |

## Index